# Her Majesty

An Illustrated Guide
to the Women
Who Ruled the World

Written & Illustrated by Lisa Graves

For Brian, who gives me free reign.

And for my young supporters:
Molly, Fallon, Taylor, Brynn, Maeve,
the Sophias, Emma, Haley, Bella, Reilly,
Lily, Charlie, Raena, Finn, Stella, Sean,
Gabrielle, and Julia.

Special thanks to Beckett Graham, Susan
Vollenweider, and Edward Branley for their
extensive knowledge and guidance.

Shown on the cover: Marie Antoinette,
Queen Consort of France and Navarre (1755 - 1793)

Hardcover ISBN: 978-1-62395-736-0
eISBN: 978-1-62395-737-7
ePib ISBN: 978-1-62395-738-4
Published in the United States
by Xist Publishing
www.xistpublishing.com

# YOU DON'T NECESSARILY NEED A CROWN
(but they sure are pretty)

The definition of queen is: a female ruler of an independent state, especially one who inherits the position by right of birth.

For most of the women in this book that definition works, but there is SO much more to the story. Many became Queen by marriage, others became Queen on behalf of a young child, and others took their throne by force! Some were peaceful leaders while some were warriors—but all faced different hardships and challenges including unpopularity, gossip, the loss of a child, betrayal, imprisonment, banishment, war, mental illness, disease, political upheavals, and much more.

From doing the research on these amazing women, it is clear to see that having money and power isn't everything and it certainly isn't the key to happiness.

How is the information in the book applicable to us today? By learning about our history, we can ensure the past doesn't repeat itself. By reading about successes and failures, about what went right and what went wrong, we can all learn valuable information that can change our world. Whether on a personal level or a global campaign – everyone can make a difference. For example, Catherine the Great established the first school for the higher education for Women in Russia. This led to educational reforms and more schools. Queen Victoria, who made the decision to wear a white wedding dress, set a global fashion trend that has withstood time. When Boudica's family was abused and mistreated by the Romans, she formed a rebellion and drove their tormentors straight out of England!

What can you do to change your world? Will you study other cultures and travel abroad? Will you chose peaceful resolutions to conflict? Will you help others to learn and grow in your community? There are many ways everyone can make a difference. You just need to decide how and when.

# Hapshepsut

**BIRTH NAME:** Hapshepsut

**REIGN:** 1479 - 1458 BC

**COUNTRY:** Ancient Egypt

**BORN:** 1508 BC

**DIED:** 1458 BC

**SPOUSE:** Thutmose II

## GREATEST ACHIEVEMENT:

Hapshepsut opened trade routes, led military campaigns, and commissioned hundreds of monuments, temples, and large construction projects during her 21-year reign. She is considered the most powerful, and most successful female Pharaoh.

Hapshepsut came from a royal family. As daughter to Thutmose I, she was born a princess. Thutmose I became Pharaoh when the previous Pharaoh did not have a son.

Her brothers and sisters died very young which left her as heir to the throne. Her father died shortly after she married, so her husband became Thutmose II. He too died young, so her nephew became Thutmose III. So many Thutmoses, it's hard to follow, but this was common practice in prominent families. Because her nephew was too young to rule at the time, Hapshepsut was in charge and declared herself Pharaoh.

She was a very strategic leader and developed trade routes that brought enormous wealth to her country.

But life was not entirely easy for a female Pharaoh. In order for people to think of her as their true leader, she constructed multiple monuments and statues of herself to ensure the people of Egypt perceived her as Pharaoh. She also dressed like a man – including a fake beard and cobra-topped headdress!

Hapshepsut sent expeditions to neighboring countries, including the land of Punt. Her explorers brought back trade goods including 31 Myrrh trees. They transported the trees by placing their roots in baskets to keep them alive. Myrrh trees were used for making perfume, incense, and medicines. It is said to have been Hapshepsut's favorite scent.

# Boudica

**BIRTH NAME:** Boudica, Boudicca, Boadicea, Buddug
**REIGN:** 48 - 61 AD
**COUNTRY:** England and Ireland
**BORN:** 30 AD
**DIED:** 61 AD
**SPOUSE:** Prasutagus
**CHILDREN:** two daughters, names unknown

**GREATEST ACHIEVEMENT:**
Boudica successfully united the tribes of England to revolt against the Romans who had occupied most of the country and tortured the residents.

## WARRIOR QUEEN

Boudica was described as having a harsh voice, piercing eyes, and thick red hair that went down past her waist. She was the Queen of The Iceni Tribe. These people occupied what is now known as Southeast England. When the Romans took over the area, the Iceni were grossly mistreated. Her people were subjected to abuse, torture, slavery, and high taxes.

When Boudica's husband, Prasutagus, died, by law his possessions were supposed to be passed over to the Roman Emperor (clearly, the Romans created that rule!). It was a terrible time. The Romans were so cruel to Boudica and her family, that a rebellion began to grow. Boudica organized the tribes and led an army against the Roman Empire and eventually drove them out of England.

The Temple of Claudius

Boudica led her army to Colchester (known then as Camulodunum). The city was poorly guarded but represented the Roman Occupation with its temple dedicated to Roman Emperor Claudius. The Iceni warriors destroyed the temple and leveled the entire city.

In 1070, long after the temple was destroyed, Colchester Castle was built on the foundation of where that temple stood.

In 1907, the head from a bronze statue of Claudius was found in the River Alde, about 30 miles from the city.

This map shows the locations of the tribes in 50 AD. Boudica was the Queen of the Icenis

Cornavii
Carini
Lugi Taexali
Cerones
Vacomagi
Venicone
Salgovae
Boidii
Votad
Novantae
Carvetii
Brigantes
Parisi
Deceangli
Coritani
Ordovices
Iceni
Demetae
Trinovantes
Silures
Catuvellauni
Cantiaci
Durotriges Regni
Dumnonii

The Britons (Celtics) were tribal people who lived in what we now call England. They were invaded by the Romans in 43 AD under Emperor Claudius. Despite Boudica's successful rebellion, they were no match for the Roman Army and were eventually defeated.

# Zenobia

Zenobia was a brave and fearless leader for her people. Palmyra had been fighting for their independence from Rome for some time. Zenobia retaliated in every way possible. Three different Roman emperors tried to take her down, but it was only the third, Emperor Aurelian, that made it his mission to put a stop to her rebellion. He eventually captured her and then proceeded to humiliate the Queen by parading her around the city in chains to show off his victory.

# QUEEN OF THE PALMYRENE EMPIRE

**BIRTH NAME:** Julia Aurelia Zenobia

**COUNTRY:** Palmyra (now Syria)

**BORN:** around 252 AD

**DIED:** 274 AD

**SPOUSE:** Septimius Odaenathus, King of Palmyra

**CHILDREN:**

Vaballathus, Herrennianus, Timolaus

## GREATEST ACHIEVEMENT:

After her husband's death, Zenobia ruled Palmyra on behalf of her young son, Vaballathus. She proved to be a bold and calculating leader, declaring independence from Rome, and seizing Egypt and parts of Asia. She was truly a warrior queen, personally leading her troops into battle.

Roman Emperor Aurelian ruled from 270 to 275. He rose to power through his military conquests and is credited for ending the Crisis of the Third Century. This "crisis" was led by Queen Zenobia.

Zenobia was born in Palmyra, Syria. Although we do not know her exact birth year, one could guess it would be around 252. There were claims that she was a direct descendant of Cleopatra, but there is some confusion as to WHICH Cleopatra as there were several that could have been relatives. She also said that she was a descendant of Dido, Queen of Carthage (the first Queen of what we now call Libya).

She was extremely intelligent and fluent in Greek, Egyptian, and Aramaic. After her husband died, Zenobia took charge and worked to expand Palmyra's territories. The Romans were NOT happy about this. At the Battle of Immae, the Romans finally defeated Zenobia and her troops – but she escaped. Soon after, she was captured and brought to Rome.

There are no records of what became of her. Some historians say she was executed, others say she was allowed to live for several years. We just don't know. What we do know, is that she goes down in history as one of its most notable female leaders.

## The Palmyrene Empire

The Palmyrene Empire had a short existence. Palmyra, the capital, was located in the center of what we now call Syria. The Palmyrenes, who adored Queen Zenobia, wanted to break away from the Roman Empire in hopes of becoming independent from the harsh Emperors. They were forced to give up their independence only a few years after claiming it. After being defeated in two major battles, Palmyra was destroyed by Roman soldiers.

# Empress WU ZETIAN

曌

Empress Wu, along with her many other contributions to her people, introduced new words. She borrowed elements from an ancient language to create new ways of communicating. She was also an accomplished poet. The symbol above was her name which translates to "Illuminate."

**BIRTH NAME:** Wu Mei, Wu Zhao

**REIGN:** 655-683 AD

**COUNTRY:** China

**BORN:** February 17, 624 AD

**DIED:** December 16, 705 AD

**SPOUSE:** Emperor Taizon of Tang, Emporer Gaozong of Tang

**CHILDREN:**

Li Hong, Emperor of Yizong

Li Xian, Crown Prince Zhanghuai

Princess Si of Anding

Li Xian, Emperor Zhongzong

Li Dan, Emperor Ruizong

Princess Taiping

**GREATEST ACHIEVEMENT:**

Developed agriculture and irrigation systems, ordered the development of farming development and education. In doing so, she enabled systems that allowed peasant farmers to generate successful crops.

# MOTHER KNOWS BEST

Wu Zetian was the only female in Chinese history to rule as emperor in her own right. Impressive.

She was born as Wu Zhao in what is now known as Guangyuan City. Her family was well-off due to a close relationship with Emperor Gaozu of Tang. She had servants and was encouraged to read and educate herself. She became a secretary to the emperor when she was fourteen which allowed her to continue her education.

She became Empress Consort of the Tang Dynasty and ruled from 655 to 683. In her efforts to be accepted by Confucian leaders, she started a campaign to elevate the position of women by having scholars write biographies of famous women, raised the position of her mother's clan, and gave her relatives high political posts.

Her core belief was that the ideal ruler was one who ruled like a mother.

This map shows the extent of Wu Zetian's vast empire.

The region extended over the countries now known as China, Laos and Vietnam.

# EMPRESS IRENE

**BIRTH NAME:** Irene Sarantapechaina

**REIGN:** 797- 802 AD

**COUNTRY:** Greece

**BORN:** 752

**DIED:** 803

**SPOUSE:** Leo IV

**CHILDREN:** Constantine VI

## GREATEST ACHIEVEMENT:

Restoring the religious practice of using icons, or religious images, in the Christian church. Worshipping these images had been banned for over sixty years. She was also the first woman to rule the Byzantine Empire and was instrumental in promoting the silk trade.

## THE BYZANTINE EMPIRE

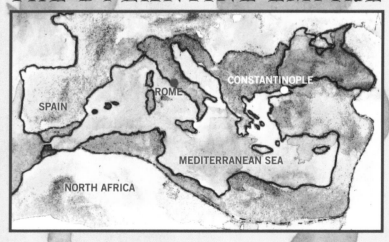

## THE QUEEN OF MEAN

Irene was related to a very noble family from Athens, but she was an orphan. It is unclear how she came to marry the Emperor's son Leo, but some say she was chosen in a "bride-show." These shows were essentially "auditions" in which eligible young ladies would be presented to the Emperor in hopes of becoming his daughter-in-law.

Irene's rise to power did not come without controversy. When her own son was named emperor, she had him attacked and imprisoned, thus proving him to be unworthy of the title. This strategic and somewhat evil maneuver allowed her to reign supreme for the next five years.

Irene was known to love imported silk so much that she developed her own factories in Greece. The workers in her silk factories were held as prisoners (Irene feared they would be kidnapped by other countries trying to profit from the production of their own silks). Because of this, historians describe her as a very cruel and aggressive ruler.

She was eventually kicked off her throne, sent to the Greek Island of Lesbos, and stripped of all power. She died one year later.

The gold coin made during her short reign was marked with the word "Basilissa" (Empress).

Constantinople was the first silk-weaving city in Europe. During Irene's reign, silks were often used as a form of payment for other goods.

Byzantine silks were unique because of their bright colors and hints of gold thread. Irene was very fond of these beautiful textiles and wore them for special events including a trip to Athens for her wedding in 769 AD.

# Empress Matilda

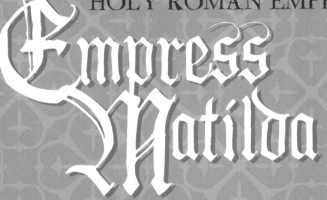

Empress Matilda was the daughter of King Henry I of England. When her brother William was killed, Henry was left with no male heir to the throne. So before he died, he made his chief noblemen swear to accept Matilda as their Queen. However, when Henry did pass, these noblemen took back their promise and Matilda's cousin Stephen of Blois took the throne. After several violent battles, Stephen was imprisoned and Matilda did, in fact, take over.

She had a very bad temper and did not treat her people well. Stephen's wife begged for Matilda to release him from prison, but Matilda refused. This came back to haunt her because Stephen's army came and stormed Oxford Castle. She escaped, dressing all in white to disguise herself in the snow, climbing down the walls by rope, and fleeing to Wallingford, England. She was never officially crowned Queen, but rather given the title "Lady of the English." Her son did become King of England as Henry II. His reign lasted 35 years.

**BIRTH NAME:** Maude

**REIGN:** April 1141 - November 1141 AD

**COUNTRY:** Holy Roman Empire

**BORN:** February 7, 1102 AD

**DIED:** September 10, 1167 AD

**SPOUSE:** Henry V, Geoffrey V

**CHILDREN:**

Henry II of England

Geoffrey, Count of Nantes

William X, Count of Poitou

**GREATEST ACHIEVEMENT:**

Matilda was known to have a vicious temper, however, one could say it would take an intimidating person to be the only woman to take over the throne of England during the middle ages. She also ensured that her son, Henry (King Henry II), would become King after the death of King Stephen.

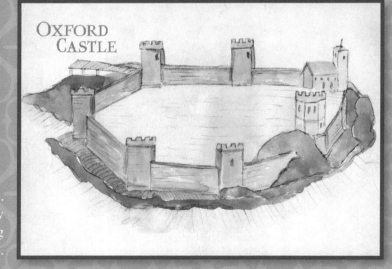

OXFORD CASTLE

Oxford Castle was a formidable fortress. Most of it was destroyed in the 18th century but some of the structure is still standing in Oxfordshire, England.

Matilda spent her later years at a convent in Normandy, France, where she continued to be somewhat involved with political decisions and representing her son, Henry.

When she died, whatever she had left was given to the church. She was buried in a tomb that had the inscription "Great by birth, greater by marriage, greatest in her offspring: here lies Matilda, the daughter, wife, and mother of Henry."

Isabella's daughter, Joanna

Isabella's half-brother, Henry IV, was not happy about her choice to marry Ferdinand. He had chosen Alfonso V. His selections for her were very self-serving and were just an attempt to control the very powerful Isabella.

King Ferdinand II (1452-1516) supported his wife in almost every decision. They even had a prenuptial agreement in which they laid out terms of their equality in the marriage. He passed away twelve years after Isabella, leaving Spain in the incapable hands of his daughter Joanna.

Joanna was often referred to as Joanna the Mad because she was mentally ill. What a terrible nickname to stay with you throughout history. She was treated at a convent for what was most likely a condition called schizophrenia.

# Isabella I of Castile

As the daughter of John II of Castile, Isabella advanced to the throne by birth-right. At the age of 18, she chose her husband, Ferdinand. The two had a long and happy relationship. The decision to marry Ferdinand united the very turbulent country of Spain and brought together the kingdoms of Castile and Aragon. In 1492 she sponsored Christopher Columbus's trip to the Americas which brought the Spaniards enormous wealth and discoveries. This period of time was called the Golden Age for Spain.

Unfortunately, her reign is marked by the decision to banish all of her citizens that refused to convert to Catholicism, causing an outbreak of turmoil and violence. Although she was successful in stifling these confrontations, her popularity amongst her people waned.

She had five children, but two of them died during her lifetime. A sixth (and twin to Maria) was stillborn. Her daughter Joanna was mentally ill. Catherine, her youngest, was the first wife of King Henry VIII. Catherine had a daughter with Henry that grew up to be Queen Mary I of England (half-sister of Queen Elizabeth I.)

**BIRTH NAME:** Isabella
**REIGN:** 1474-1504 AD
**COUNTRY:** Spain
**BORN:** April 22, 1451 AD
**DIED:** November 26, 1504 AD
**SPOUSE:** Ferdinand II, King of Aragon
**CHILDREN:**
Isabella, Queen of Portugal
John, Prince of Austria
Joanna, Queen of Castile & Aragon
Maria, Queen of Portugal
Catherine, Queen of England

**GREATEST ACHIEVEMENT:**
Sponsoring Columbus' voyage to the Americas, transitioning Spain from Medieval to Modern, and for mothering four future Queens!

The Arms of King Ferdinand and Queen Isabella

# Queen Elizabeth I

**BIRTH NAME:** Elizabeth Tudor
**REIGN:** 1558 - 1603 AD
**COUNTRY:** England and Ireland
**BORN:** September 7, 1533 AD
**DIED:** March 24, 1603 AD
**SPOUSE:** None
**CHILDREN:** None

### GREATEST ACHIEVEMENT:

Elizabeth defeated the Spanish Armada, an epic event for the times. This helped to establish England as a political and military powerhouse.

She was incredibly dedicated to her people. Her reign is known as the Elizabethan Era. She loved and encouraged the arts and provided stability for her country for over forty years.

The Tudors were a Welsh-English family that ruled England and Wales from 1485 to 1603. Henry VII was the first Tudor King followed by King Henry VIII, Edward VI, Mary I (Elizabeth's half-sister) and Elizabeth I.

The Tudor dynasty was well known for colorful characters and their impact on English history.

The Tudor Rose (shown to the left) is a very famous symbol representing their 116 year dynasty.

Elizabeth's official signature

## THE GOOD QUEEN BESS

Along with her father, King Henry VIII, Elizabeth is probably one of England's most well-known monarchs. Her childhood was very troublesome as her mother was executed by her father when Elizabeth was only two. Despite her tumultuous early years she grew up to be one of the most powerful women in history.

After the death of her half-sister, Queen Mary I, Elizabeth took the throne at the age of 25. It is believed that due to her first-hand account of difficult royal marriages, Elizabeth decided not to marry. She had many suitors who sought to gain religious and political power, but she never accepted any of their proposals. She became "married" to her country and her people. Because of this dedication, she earned the nickname, the "Virgin Queen."

King Henry VIII

Queen Anne Boleyn

Father

Mother

Elizabeth's Mother, Anne Boleyn, was the second wife of King Henry VIII. Although he loved his daughter Elizabeth, he really wanted a son as heir to the throne. Because Anne was unable to give birth to a healthy boy, Henry considered their marriage cursed and had Elizabeth's mother brought up on false charges so he could seek a divorce. He married his third wife just twelve days after Anne was executed.

*Though the sex to which I belong is considered weak, you will nevertheless find me a rock that bends to no wind.*
QUEEN ELIZABETH I

# Catherine II of Russia

Catherine married Grand Duke Peter on January 5, 1762. When Peter's Aunt Elizabeth Petrovna died, her nephew became Emperor of Russia with Catherine as his Consort.

Peter was a very unpopular ruler and quickly abdicated the throne. He was assassinated soon after, making Catherine the sole ruler of Russia (and she wasn't even Russian!). Rumors circulated, but there is no proof she had anything to do with her husband's death.

Peter III of Russia

**The Imperial Crown of Russia** was made specifically for Catherine's Coronation by her Court Jeweler. Its design contains 4,936 diamonds! It is currently on display in Moscow.

# CATHERINE THE GREAT

Catherine, born Sophie Friederike, changed her name so that it would be more "Russian" after being carefully selected as the wife of Grand Duke Peter. She even changed her religion in order to be properly welcomed by the people of her new country.

While these changes won her some popularity with the Russian Nobles, they did not lead to a happy marriage. Peter and Catherine led very separate lives and eventually she proved to be the more powerful monarch.

As she rose to power, gossip followed Catherine everywhere – even after her death. Her life of extreme wealth and control also had some quirks—she forbade yawning and sighing as well as boring people and drunkards! Visitors were to conduct any arguments behind closed doors, weapons were to be left outside, and women were not allowed to wear dresses that might be prettier than hers!

Unfortunately, Catherine is remembered in history for her scandalous personal life rather than her political achievements. Power isn't everything!

**BIRTH NAME: Sophie Friederike Auguste, Prinzessin von Anhalt-Zerbst**
**REIGN: 1762-1796 AD**
**COUNTRY: Russia**
**BORN: May 2, 1729 AD**
**DIED: November 17, 1796 AD**
**SPOUSE: Peter III of Russia**

**GREATEST ACHIEVEMENT:**

Catherine modernized Russia – her reign is called Russia's Golden Age. New towns and cities were developed, the empire expanded, and she established the first institute of higher learning for women, the Smolny Institute. Her tenure was not without controversy as nobles benefited the most from her decisions while the lower class suffered and were mistreated.

**BIRTH NAME:** Duchess Louise Auguste Wilhelmine Amalie of Mecklenburg-Strelitz

**REIGN:** 1797-1810 AD

**COUNTRY:** Prussia

**BORN:** March 10, 1776 AD

**DIED:** July 19, 1810 AD

**SPOUSE:** Frederick William III

**CHILDREN:**

Frederick William IV, King of Prussia

William I, German Emperor

Alexandra Feodorovna, Empress of Russia

Princess Frederica

Prince Charles

Alexandrine, Grand Duchess of Mecklenburg-Schwerin

Prince Ferdinand

Louise, Princess Frederick of the Netherlands

Prince Albert

**GREATEST ACHIEVEMENT:**

Louise was loved and respected by her people. She was influential on all matters of state. When she passed away suddenly at the age of 34, Napoleon commented that the king had "lost his best minister."

The Order of Louise was an honor bestowed upon women of Germany for outstanding service to their country. It was founded by Louise's husband, King Frederick William III of Prussia, as a tribute to his late wife.

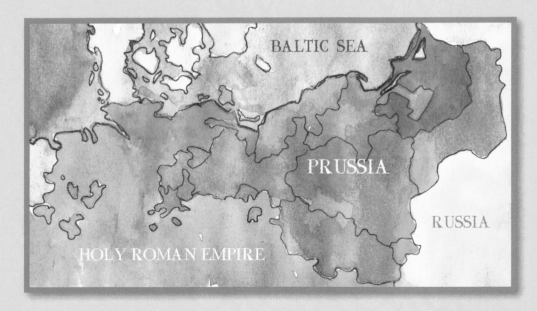

These were tumultuous times in this part of the world. Prussia's borders were in constant turmoil and changed quite a bit in the years that followed Louise's death.

Today this area is broken up into Poland and Germany.

# Queen Louise
## of Mecklenburg-Strelitz

## QUEEN CONSORT OF PRUSSIA
## ELECTRESS CONSORT
## OF BRANDENBURG

Louise was the daughter of Prince Charles of Mecklenburg-Strelitz. When she was only six years old, her mother passed away while giving birth to Louise's sister. After their father remarried, his new wife (and Louise's aunt) died while giving birth to a son. Because of these difficult times, Louise and her two sisters were sent to live with her grandmother. Her brothers remained with their father.

While under the care of her grandmother, Louise was well educated with lessons in history, languages, and the arts.

She met her husband on March 14, 1793 and married later that year. The people of Germany fell in love with her immediately. In November of 1797, Frederick became King and Louise was thrown into the busy life of royalty. She did this well, as her subjects adored her for her grace, charm, beauty, and sense of fashion!

# LAKSHMIBAI

India's struggle for freedom from British Rule continued after Lakshmibai's death. The movement for independence was led by a very peaceful man named Mahatma Gandhi.

Ghandi convinced the people of India to start a non-violent protest against the British. He wanted them to stop paying taxes on salt (paying these taxes caused widespread poverty amongst the people of India.)

Although he spent many years in prison for his peaceful protests, it paid off. In 1947, India was declared independent from Britain. He is referred to as the father of India and his birthday is a national holiday.

# THE RANI OF THE JHANSI

**BIRTH NAME:** Manikarnika Tambe

**COUNTRY:** India

**BORN:** November 19, 1835 AD

**DIED:** June 17, 1858 AD

**SPOUSE:** Jhansi Naresh Maharaj
Gangadhar Rao Newalkar

**CHILDREN:**

Damodar Rao

Anand Rao

## GREATEST ACHIEVEMENT:

Lakshmibai (also Lakshmi) was reluctant to be the leader of a rebellion, but when push came to shove, she put on men's clothes, got on her horse, and led her people to fight against their oppressors. To this day, she is thought of as a National Heroine.

Lakshmibai's official title was Rani of the Jhansi. Rani is a term for a Hindu Queen. She was born in Northern India to a prominent family. Her mother died when she was very young, but her father saw to her education. She was trained in horsemanship, fencing, and shooting.

She married Gangadhar Rao Newalkar when she was very young and took the name of Lakshmibai. They had one son, who died in infancy, but adopted a 5-year-old distant cousin. Tragically, Gangadhar died the day after the adoption went through. So Lakshmi served as Rani on behalf of their adopted son.

At this time, the British government controlled most of India. They did not approve of Lakshmibai serving as Rani and claimed that they would seize control of Jhansi.

Lakshmi protested their decisions on several occasions, but her letters were ignored and then rejected. Violence erupted against the British, and eventually a resistance formed. The British blamed Lakshmi for the revolt. She escaped from her home, but her father was captured and executed.

Heartbroken, but driven to defend her people, Lakshmi dressed in men's clothes and led a group of her people out to fight the British. After two days of battle she was shot and killed. The leader of the British troops, Sir Hugh Rose said "The Rani is remarkable for her bravery, cleverness and perseverance; her generosity to her subordinates was unbounded. These qualities, combined with her rank, rendered her the most dangerous of all the rebel leaders."

Victoria was married on February 10, 1840 to Albert of Saxe-Coburg and Gotha. She wore a white wedding dress and is credited for starting the global tradition of brides wearing white. Her 12 bridesmaids also wore white.

# Queen Victoria

**BIRTH NAME:** Alexandrina Victoria

**REIGN:** 1837-1901 AD

**COUNTRY:** United Kingdom

**BORN:** May 24, 1819 AD

**DIED:** January 22, 1901 AD

**SPOUSE:**

**Albert of Saxe-Coburg and Gotha**

## GREATEST ACHIEVEMENT:

Victoria survived six assassination attempts, created the concept of a "family monarchy," and almost all of her children went on to have prominent roles in world politics. She was even given the nickname "the Grandmother of Europe" having nine children, 40 grand-children, and 37 great-grandchildren.

The current Queen Elizabeth II and her husband, the Duke of Edinburgh, are both Victoria's great-great-grandchildren.

**PRINCE EDWARD**
DUKE OF KENT AND STRATHEARN

**PRINCESS VICTORIA**
OF SAXE-COBURG-SAATFELD

**QUEEN VICTORIA**

**ALBERT**
OF SAXE-COBURG AND GOTHA

| | |
|---|---|
| **VICTORIA** PRINCESS ROYAL, GERMAN EMPRESS | Was crowned Princess Royal of the UK in 1841. Also became German Empress and Queen of Prussia by marriage. (1840-1901) |
| **EDWARD VII** | King of the UK and the British Dominions as well as Emperor of India. He was considered to be a peacemaker. (1841-1910) |
| **PRINCESS ALICE** GRAND DUCHESS OF HESSE | Married Louis IV, Grand Duke of Hesse and had 7 children. Her descendants went on to play major roles in world history. (1843-1878) |
| **ALFRED** DUKE OF SAXE-COBURG AND GOTHA | Married Grand Duchess Maria Alexandrovna of Russia, daughter of Alexander II of Russia. (1844-1900) |
| **HELENA** PRICESS CHRISTIAN OF SCHLESWIG-HOLSTEIN | Helena was devoted to the nursing profession and loved music. She had 5 children. (1846-1923) |
| **PRINCESS LOUISE** DUCHESS OF ARGYLL | Full name Louise Caroline Alberta, The province of Alberta, Canada was named after her as well as Lake Louise and Mount Alberta. (1848-1939) |
| **PRINCE ARTHUR** DUKE OF CONNAUGHT | Served as the Governor General of Canada and served in the British Army for over 40 years. (1850-1942) |
| **PRINCE LEOPOLD** DUKE OF ALBANY | Died at age 30 from Hemophilia, a deadly blood condition sometimes called "The Royal Disease" (1853-1884) |
| **BEATRICE** PRINCESS OF BATTENBERG | The last of Queen Victoria's children to die, she married Prince Henry of Battenberg and had four children. (1857-1944) |

Victoria was the first monarch to live at Buckingham Palace in London. She was highly educated, spoke several languages, and kept extensive journals, writing over 2,500 words a day in those journals! When her husband died in 1861, she went into a permanent state of mourning. She wore only black for the rest of her life. She was kind and considerate, influential in political affairs, and loved going to the opera. Her reign over the United Kingdom is called the Victorian Era; a time of peace, prosperity, and cultural growth in British history.

# Tsarina Alexandra

**BIRTH NAME:** Alix of Hesse

**REIGN:** 1894 - 1917 AD

**COUNTRY:** Russia

**BORN:** June 6, 1872 AD

**DIED:** July 17, 1918 AD

**SPOUSE:** Nicholas II of Russia

**CHILDREN:**

Grand Duchess Olga Nikolaevna
Grand Duchess Tatiana Nikolaevna
Grand Duchess Maria Nikolaevna
Grand Duchess Anastasia Nikolaevna
Tsarevich Alexei Nikolaevich

Many rumors circulated throughout the world that Alexandra's youngest daughter, Anastasia, had survived the execution. This rumor became the subject of many books and movies. However, after extensive testing and research, scientists concluded that she did not survive.

Her full name was Alexandra Feodorovna Romanova, and her story is quite sad. She married the last Tsar of Russia, Nicholas, on November 26, 1894 and was officially crowned as Empress of Russia two years later. She was a very shy and private person, but the people of Russia misunderstood and assumed that Alexandra was just rude! They had five children, but her son suffered from a fatal blood disease. In desperation, Alexandra sought the help of a holy man named Grigori Rasputin who claimed to have a cure. He, unfortunately, was a fraud that took advantage of poor Alexandra, who only wanted to heal the very sick Alexei.

Due to the political turmoil surrounding World War I, Russia's Royal Family was overthrown, kidnapped and eventually executed. The entire family was assassinated in a prison basement. Over the years the case has been extensively investigated because there were claims that Alexandra's daughter Anastasia survived the execution. This, however, was proven to be false in 2010 through DNA testing.

Grigori Rasputin claimed to be a faith healer and conned his way into being a private adviser to Alexandra and her family. Historians believe that it was his influence over the Romanov family that led to their ultimate demise.

The women in this book have well-documented histories both at your local library and online. For further research, ask your librarian for books that feature a specific Queen or Empress. There were so many interesting and courageous women in history it was difficult to select who would be featured in this book. Additional women you may consider researching could include: Marie Antoinette (shown on the cover), Christina of Sweden, Queen Amina, Lady Jane Grey, Queen Mary I, Mary Queen of Scots, Elizabeth of York, Queen Wilhemina, or Cleopatra!

Some links to help you get started:
historyforkids.net
bbc.co.uk/history/forkids/
thehistorychicks.com
accessible-archives.com
thefreelancehistorywriter.com


The Women in History Series, written and illustrated by Lisa Graves
also includes:
*History's Witches, An Illustrated Guide*
*Trail Blazers, An Illustrated Guide to the Women Who Explored the World*


About the Author
Lisa Graves is an illustrator, author, history buff, and mom to two creative children. She lives in Massachusetts with her family and her dog, Henry. Lisa is the creator of historywitch.com. You can see more of her illustrations at lisagravesdesign.com